Crescendo of Chaos

Victoria Lauren

Crescendo of Chaos is dedicated to anyone who has ever felt like they are too much, anyone who accidentally fell in love with the world around them before realizing how sharp it can be, and for anyone who has wished upon a shooting star to be brave enough to be themselves. This is a book for all the dreamers who ache for all the lives they will never get to live.

CONTENTS

Now........1

Lifeblood........2

Sailing Home........4

Diet of a Sad Girl........6

No........7

Hey There Stranger........9

Yellow Wallpaper Girl........10

Daydreams of Grandeur........13

God of Wrath........14

Quiet Moon........16

Etiquette Lessons........17

Sand in A Glass........18

Fortissimo........19

Feast........21

Fairytale Clocks........23

Not Mine........24

Crescendo of Chaos........26

Tuesday Night Magic........28

Fork Ran Away With The Spoon........29

Empty Frames........30

Roses and Rot........31

Untied........32

My Little Sister Is Taller........33

Turning....................35
Party Dresses and Ghostly Goodbyes....................36
Least Favorite Perfume....................37
Sunshine & Waves....................39
Woman in Mourning....................40
Clutching....................41
Gleaned....................42
Forest Fires....................43
Sacred Spaces....................44
Taffy Days....................45
Rattle....................47
Oh So Delicate....................48
I Want Everything....................49
Stargazer....................50
Cliffside....................51
Diary of an Almost....................52
Sugar Pie Honey Bunch....................53
Starshine....................54
Echoes....................55
Jump....................56
Warning Symbols....................57
Radically Alive....................58
Holy Palmers Too....................60
Heavy....................61
Nothing Left for You....................62
Drunk Girls in A Bathroom....................64
Paths divulged in a wood, right?....................65

Don't Wake the Beasts....66
Witches....68
Chilled to My Bones....69
Honey & Moonlight....70
Daylight....71

& Then....72

End Credits....73
Demanding Little Headstrong Girl....74
Smoke & Mirrors....75
Lightning....77
Bonfire Memories....78
Tightropes....80
Left Wondering....83
Blood Pressure....84
Rotting Teeth....85
Tombstones....89
Small....90
Envelopes Handled with Care....92
Eclipse....93
Stale....94
Over the River....95
Acid Rain....97
Saltwater....98
Another Sunset....99
Admit It....100
Not the Careful-est of Girls....101

Sugar Lies 103
Toothache 104
Say It Again, I Dare You 105
Locket Full of Love 108
Maps 109
Ghost Summer 110
Poison on Your Lips 111
Nighttime Prayers 114
Deals with the Devil 115
Kaleidoscope Girl 116
Quiet Truths 118
Grocery Store Eggs 119
Windy Day 121
Lack of Humor 122
Bottles From the Sea 123
Empty Hands 125
Heavy Hymnals 127
Spiderwebs 128
Soda 129
Spit 130
Searchlight 131
What's My Cue Again? 132
Weak Coffee 133

Acknowledgments 136

Now

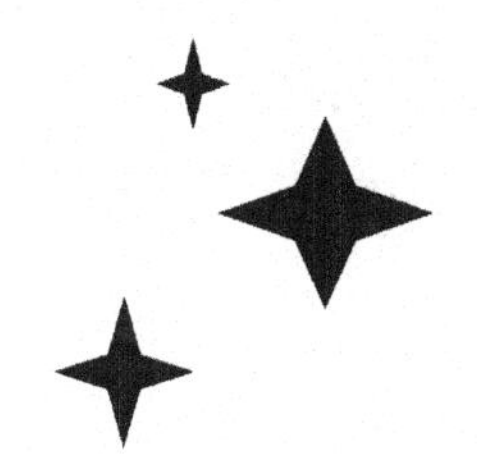

Lifeblood

I am made of seaweed and gravel,
flickering candlelight and crisp fall mornings,
raindrops splashing onto windshields mixed with quiet symphonies
of chatter from the backseat,

Made of the saltwater of tears
and the metallic ting of blood when you nick yourself shaving from
daydreaming again.

I'm made from the wrong combination of notes at the piano,
and smoky rooms full of people I love.
Consist of the low hum of crashing waves
and dappled light through the leaves of the trees,
with a dash of silk on freshly scrubbed skin.

Sunshine on your bruises
and kisses on your eyelashes.

Made from the smell of old books
and sun-faded Polaroids
Forgotten stuffed animals
and light summer dresses.

The memory box stored in the attic,
always slightly smelling of childhood summers by the lake
and tinged with the fondness of half-forgotten dreams.

I have frost in my bones and flames licking up my veins.

I am abandoned overgrown gardens and wooded winding pathways
Fresh notebooks in the fall
Jack-o-lanterns by the doorstep
and the steam rising off your coffee.
Wild flowers in the meadow
and night lights in the hallways.

The wistful remembrances of fading love bites on your neck
and long-healed scars on your chest
A combination of forehead kisses
and the feeling you get when you find your old favorite movie on television in the middle of the night.

I'm the faded strip of noir films
and the sharp edges of comic strips.

The melancholy feeling of my childhood bedroom,
gasping and drowning in leftover sadness I thought I gave away long ago.

I am moonlight and a lost madrigals song.
overly-bright sunshine and a stars last gasping breath.

Sailing Home

Sometimes I feel like a ship lost at sea
Heaving
Tilting
Listing
Lolling
Wave by wave crashing

And I'm just weathering.
Not thriving
Just surviving

Holding my breath
Waiting for calmer seas
And kinder skies

Howling winds beat my sails
Pounding waves spit me out
Twirling and swirling in all this chaos
I'm merely weathering this storm.

Sometimes I wonder if this will be the whirlpool that sinks me
If this will crack the hull
To let the bone-chilling seawater slosh inside

Some of my wood is rotting
But I patch as quickly as I can

The steering wheel careening
Spinning as fast as my heart pounds
My hands are raw from wrenching
Looking for a safer path to sail.

Diet of a Sad Girl

Pills for breakfast
Tears for lunch
This is the recipe
Of a girl who feels too much

No

What a blessing
The word
No
Is in life

How nice it is
To get exactly what I didn't know I wanted

What a lovely thing it is
To not get what I did

How lucky am I

That my wants got rejected.

And instead I got what I needed
And never thought I deserved.

Your no
Kicked off so much beauty in my life
I would have never had
Had you simply said yes

Thank god
I didn't get what I wanted

Thank god
I didn't get what I begged for

Thank god
I got the whole world instead.

Hey There Stranger

This might be the first and last time you see me
Me in my red coat tucked up tight
You with your sneaker laces coming undone
Both of us crossing
Catching eyes for just a moment
The glittering golden hour light
Making everything a bit more beautiful

And who knows
We all weave around each other
I might see you again
In a week
Or a month
Or five years
Or every day at the subway platform
Or never again

We are all orbiting and circling and bumping into and off of one another
Quietly cycling
Cycling
Cycling through.

Yellow Wallpaper Girl

I wonder if I was born sad
This deep heavy ache in the heart
Preinstalled
Like the weather app on your phone
Part of my code
Part of my package

This
That is my slight-hysterical-tendency
This aching
This longing
This fear

I can't remember a time
It wasn't in
Every
Single
Heartbeat

There are times I wonder if these walls and gates
exist solely to keep me in,
So my sorrow doesn't seep out
And infect the whole world

This wallpaper of my melancholy
Firmly stuck in place
Never quite all peeled away
No matter how long you work at it

No one who hasn't experienced these feelings
Ever believes
Their torture

The women who have gone before me
Down this garden path watered with tears
Know this wallpaper well
This garish state we were born into
Becoming nothing but a cliché
A whispered warning to those not to end up like us.

I walk the length of my cell
Kissing the wallpaper
Trying to turn it into something lovely
Instead of something wicked
If I love it enough will it change?
Can I ever see this wallpaper as anything but the women gone mad before me?
My hands don't wait for answers
They pick, pick, pick
Tearing and shredding and yanking away
Piece by yellow piece
I try and I try and I try
To peel away the sadness until my fingers bleed
One day I
Pick the cheeriest color I could ever imagine

And I paint and roll and scrape and gnaw
Until all I can possibly see
Is this new color
Happiness personified
Not a drop of yellow wallpaper to be found

No evil misery here
No pitying glances
No watchful women left

Until then,
My heart in my throat
I catch it

Underneath the new shiny coat of paint
Deep down
The wallpaper is still there,
blinking
blinking
blinking
at my attempts
to banish it.
These women will always be with me
Watching
Waiting
That's what happens
With the women of wallpaper
It creeps into every aspect of you
It stains everything you ever touch yellow.

Daydreams of Grandeur

I feel myself tipping into you

Intrigued to look closer
Study your eyes
Your freckles
Trace your jawline from memory

Tracking your laughs and your head tilts
Finding excuses to linger and touch and grab hands
Feeling anchored to you
Feeling at home in your presence

How did this happen
When did you go from a person
To a dream of mine
Wrapped up in a great big bow
Of possibility

I have so many hopes when I look at you
Soft smiles and little sighs
Have me daydreaming again

God of Wrath

My rage can level towns
Like a Greek god
Don't dare tempt me
I'll swallow your fate

Don't dare tempt me
God of Wrath
I'll flick my wrist
And write you out of my life

Our string will sever
Our words cut short
I'm not one for goodbyes
I'm not one for longing

God of Wrath
Anger boiling inside me
Fury seeping out my fingertips
Let me act now and think later

My hothead always steaming
Stomach not in knots like it was once upon a time
Displeasure has melted them all away
Leaving cool and smooth steel behind in its wake

The rough edges of regret
Scorched
Take a new shape
Where my heart used to rest

Don't tempt me
I don't flee
Don't tempt me
I stand firm
Don't tempt me
To burn another bridge
I've decimated worlds for less words

I do it as casually as breathing
As simply as smiling
And as quickly as a moment

Quiet Moon

The moon has seen my heartbreak
The moon has seen my triumph
The moon has watched

Me tumble
Tumble
Down

Knocked my head once or twice

The moon has heard my crying, pleading voice
Begging for more
Begging for less
Begging to stay the same

The moon has seen me wax and wane
Along with her

I push and pull tides too
Just the ones around me
But still all the same.

Etiquette Lessons

Dreadful etiquette I apologize
You said as you slipped through the window of my heart
buying entrance tickets with Slurpees and licorice ropes
and dazzling me
with words of wonder

Life isn't always like an 80s film
But sometimes it is
And in that summer montage
We had fireworks and coffee dates
movie screens and rain storms

Your dark jacket matched your hair
My bright lips matched the sunset
For that moment we dazzled
Before the film reel slipped

I loathe a dreadful ending.

Sand in A Glass

The stars are singing to me
A solid lullaby
Of years stacked upon years

Reminding me that as big as I feel
I'm just an ant

I'm a speck

I'm a pin point

Of a moment in time

Of a small section
Of a big universe
That kisses me goodnight
That pulls me tight
And keeps spinning
Spinning
On
On
Onward.

I'm small
I'm smaller
I'm smaller
I'm smallest
I'm a second

I'm a gasp

Fortissimo

So you're 25 and still alive
And staring right into the sun

Everything feels fast and loud and unbearably slow
You are the oldest you have ever been
And the youngest you'll ever be
All at once

And you feel that dichotomy in your chest
It rocks you to the core

This is a period of life
That jolts you to your bones

The electroshock of being alive
Never more apparent
Than the full and dull pulse pulse pulse at the base of your throat

You're 25 and still alive
And truly not quite sure how

You spent so many years toying with death
That you never planned to get this far

25 is both impossibly young and impossibly old
Depending on who you ask
Depending on the situation

I've lived a million lifetimes in one
Through books and song and lore and love
But the unraveling of time
Frays my nerves
The whooshing as it rushes past me
Stresses me past what's safe

Is there ever enough time for all the dreaming you want to do?

Feast

I will not beg for scraps of affection
I demand
A mountain of it.

I will not implore you
To see
Who I really am

If you don't
Then keep moving
Don't dare linger your eyes on me

I will not settle
For someone
Who simply wants to fuck me
Seeing me through lustful eyes and hungry hands
Viewing me as curves and caresses and curls

No

I will only allow the one who worships me
Body and soul
To lay their hands on me

To stroll into my heart
To honestly communicate with our souls.

I will not beg for your scraps

I am a whole damn feast

Fairytale Clocks

The clocks in my house are made of fairy tales
Their times never true
but twisted up stories they weave
Stately and decorated and convincing lies
Each one vastly different

I check,
I check,
Then check again.
We all know threes are powerful in fairy land.

Disconcerting and shiny and twinkling
The clock faces tell their untruths

Glittery and convincing and unrelenting
Each one separate from the other
Holding their smiles behind blasé facades
Ticking ticking ticking away

Not Mine

I remember days where butterflies sparkled in me at the sound of your name
I remember the moment butterflies turned to anvils
Thudding down to the root of me
My very core carrying the grief

Feet heavy I drag myself through it, onward and forward still
Finally, with every step
I feel lighter

One day I will speak your name
Without the taste of pennies in my mouth

I thought I saw you once
And my heart leapt
into my throat

Every word I had saved for you
Every scream,
Every question,
Every thank you,
Vowel,
And exclamation point
Died on my lips

I suddenly just felt
One feeling drop to my chest
Covering everything else neatly in that moment

Fond remembrance tugged my face up
My eyes widened
But when I opened my mouth to speak your name
You turned and
It wasn't you at all

It was just another sad boy
With long dark hair
And a deep black jacket
Haunting a place that we used to go

And in that moment, I felt
Relief and sadness
Waltzing together inside my of chest

We met eyes
and I smiled,
As we passed close enough to touch.

Crescendo of Chaos

My palms itch whenever I see a fire alarm.
The urge to pull it nearly sweeps me away
I get caught up in the glimmering idea of breaking the fragile glass
Curving my fingers around the handle
And yanking sharply
To alert and alarm
Everyone around.

It's not that I want a fire
No, I don't wish to summon disaster
But with this raging inferno clawing at my throat
I wonder how the room around me is still standing

It takes everything in me not to pull it
Just to pull it
My hang curling around the cool metal
Flipping the switch as quick as a thought

I have had this urge
Since I was a child
I want the alarm to
Scream
Shout
Blare
Yell until its throat is bloody
For all the times I couldn't make a sound

I want the noise
I want the anger
I want every syllable and flame
I have spent years
Swallowing
Behind a smile
To pour out

Maybe then
You could not ignore
My feelings

Maybe then
I would be able to fully exhale

My palms itch whenever I see a fire alarm

To create a crescendo of chaos

Tuesday Night Magic

So let's order too much Chinese food
Open all the windows
The rain will come inside the house
But we don't mind at all
A blessed baptism from the heavens above

The lights are low, and the laughs are high
Eyes bright in candlelight
The tv babbles to itself
We dance until the dishes are clean
And we forget anything other than this.

Fork Ran Away With The Spoon

Sometimes
I can feel my heart straining to get out of my chest
Yearning and tugging me
My arms itch
Wanting to pull the whole world
Close to my chest

Pull it in
Hug it close
Closer
Closer
Closer
To hold it for one quiet moment
And just have everyone be okay

For one single moment
To let us all rest

My heart is trying to
Run away with me again
Like the fork ran away with the spoon.

Empty Frames

I think given enough time I can be sad about just about anything.
This week I noticed empty picture frames.
Littered, scattered, absolutely everywhere.
Precious keepsake hopes bought and put on a shelf, waiting for a moment special enough to go inside.
The moments never came.
More and more empty frames stack up.

How can you lose something you didn't have?
You didn't create a memory good enough to print.
A solidified moment never appeared.

Roses and Rot

There's the slight taste of death in my mouth
That metallic twinge
That earthy silt
That mourning rot
It sits on my tongue and heavier on my heart.

I can taste where I've been
Paths I've walked
Or didn't
And I don't know which is worse.

I can feel the ghosts of hands I've held
The whispers of past voices floating across my skin like the gossamer of silk
The lightest brush of the heaviest emotion.
It's tricky
This dichotomy of feelings.

Untied

I am set up to wander
And wonder
And love
And express that.

I am set up to explore
To be cradled to sleep in the lap of lullabies from the oceans shore

My Little Sister Is Taller

Everything my sister touches becomes sun stained,
a little faded, somehow smelling of salt water miles and miles from the beach.
Looks like it was dropped in a lake and dragged through the mud.
Like it's been to endless parties and soirées and now at daybreak it yawns, tired, about to head to bed, full of loads of good stories to tell but choosing not to.
It's all a little mussed but distinctly hers.
Off on quiet adventures and sundrenched days returning home only when it's down to the last few dollars, sunburned and scorched, to recharge and head out again.

Just like her
All her items start out brightly colored and fresh, but softly blur together, the brightness fading into a sun-kissed color all of its own.
A muted summer color.

She was supposed to be my little sister, but she burned brighter.
Louder. Stronger.
She didn't speak much and never when she didn't want to but when she did it was either witty or wise.
Sharp tongued she burst with her emotions, never just talking, instead shouting her thoughts and jokes.; as blunt as the perfect ends of her hair.
At sundown she came alive, blooming into who she really was, awakening when the lights came on. She would swirl out and I would watch her go off into the night, a silent waltz.

I never saw her go to bed. I never stayed up that late. I kept quiet in the mornings, lights dim, and cabinets shut lightly. She would drift in early afternoon, awake for another day, never eating breakfast foods, skipping the morning and skipping its meal. She preferred what the rest of the day had to offer.

Fueled for her next adventures she would drift out in a cloud of hairspray and my "borrowed" perfume, makeup lovingly applied already somehow looking like a photograph.

She would glide off into the night, towards lights and friends and things I knew little about. But the air of those nights clung to her, gossamer light, the summer air drenched into her hair and wrapped in her clothes and washing all her bright colors together, creating her very own shade of blurred and faded primary colors. It was her signature. Everything a little tousled, like it was full of stories to tell, but only if you asked the right questions.

Turning

Does the sky ever turn
that wonderful
blinding
blue?
Full of fluffy clouds,
perfect fall leaves flying
and you feel your heart flutter,
knowing these
flitting
and fleeting moments
are too far in between,
but what make life worth living?

There.
Already the moment is gone.
The shimmering bubble popped.
How swiftly the sky turns-
and all at once
it's now grey and dripping tears.

Party Dresses and Ghostly Goodbyes

The ghosts of my past lurk behind corners and hems of party dresses
In glimpses of faces
Caught from corners of my eye

Haunting me
Hounding me
Never at my heels
But instead just out of reach

How many goodbyes have I already botched?

Is this why I constantly feel watched
There are ghosts here
I dance with them
We waltz along
To a clashing cadence
I wrap my arms around my partner
Spinning on and on
Deep into the night

Dissonance all around me
From my lips
To my fumbled steps

Ghosts graze my hair
As they slip by me
Always just out of sight,
Yet never out of mind.

Least Favorite Perfume

The perfume of death
It sticks to the skin
It swirls in the air
It dances on the tongue

It chokes you
Like a silk noose

The seasons are swift
Calendar pages flipping
Faster and faster lately

Moments that used to stretch on
You keep trying to gather
And catch in your hands
Like water you try to catch in your fingers,
It slips through quicker the more you try to hold on.

Everything lately seems all ending
No beginning

Chapters slamming
Cliffhangers jumped

But what if there are no fresh notebook pages
What if there are no sunrises
What if there is no next episode

My skin is silty
Eyes full of grit
I'm not sure how many more goodbyes
Are left in my mouth

Sunshine & Waves

You know that glittering,
dizzying,
blinding
way water gets?

How beautiful
that white crest is
on a wave.

It builds and builds
until it knocks you over.

Ferocious,
Rollicking,
Rolling.
Beautiful,
Powerful,
They'll send you right over.

Some people are like that.
Beautiful,
But you know

They're going to knock you flat.

Woman in Mourning

To be a woman
Is to help mourn

To gather tightly those you love
And absorb some of the shock
From their biggest blows

To do your best to lessen the hurt
To take on a tiny bit of the ache

To mourn with them
To mourn for them

Clutching

Do you ever feel your heart break
Do you ever feel your soul leave a little at a time
Do you ever wave at your dreams in the rearview mirror

That ache
That clutch
That hurt
Doesn't ever really fade
Or do we just learn to eat our cereal with cracks in our dreams
Remembering those long ago hopes as faded as the carpet on your back steps
Beaten by weather
Bleached by sun
Faded by the feet that walked over it on their way through

I feel like that sometimes
My soul feels as faded as an old photograph
A Polaroid yellowed at the edges
Wavy and warped
The faces just out of reach

My dreams feel like that now.

They used to be so clear.
Now they're just here.

Background noise.
A quiet ache.
Another disappointment.

Gleaned

There are so many women who built me
One lent me her kind hands to gently unravel lies
One gave me her sweet smile sheathed in perfect lipstick
From another my knife point glare

Every single bit of me
Was gleaned from someone else
Women who built me brick by brick
Over years and millennia and eons

Loaning me their wisdom
Forging my future in their quests for equality
Birthing me through their kindness

I am a work in progress
And I'll keep building
So women one day
Can keep climbing
Maybe they'll have my crisp laugh
Or perhaps my healing glow
I've never been as blessed by anything
As I have been to be a woman

Forest Fires

Sometimes even the forest
Sends fire in
To rage
To cleanse

To clear pathways
For new growth

Maybe that's how I am
Burning
To give space to new neuron pathways
The change in me so subtle
You can only tell when there's smoke coming out my ears

Sacred Spaces

That holy hush of a church
Cloaking you as you enter
Incense dragging itself across the room to greet you
Stained glass glinting
Rosaries dangling
Water bubbling

This is sacred space
The heavy silence holds you close
Dripping candle wax and your footsteps the only sound that dares
enter this blessed chamber

Fatigue settles deep into your bones
Weighing you down
Time slips off its scale
Tipping onto a new course now
Time in these hallowed places isn't real
The rules are different here.

Taffy Days

Blur.
This year has been a complete blur.
My brain is full of fog
And days fall quick and fast like snow.

It feels like one arduously long week
But the calendar says it has been nearly ten months
Everything feels both really close and really far away,
like a dream right after you wake up,
Reaching fingers out to capture the smoke
Images already half gone.

The ache is constant
And tinges everything with a tired air
Each mouthful heavy

Hope is something I remember
My pockets empty of it
I am as strong
As wet newspaper

Days stretch on like taffy
Endless
Endless
Endless
Then over like a cloud passing past the sun

My days
My weeks
My months
Blur together softly
Stacking like dry leaves ready to blow away
Washed together like rain on a windshield
Drifting together like snow

I am still here
I'm soft
Cloudy
Coming apart at the edges
But I am still here.

Rattle

My body creaks
Stasis long set in
I can't remember moving
Bending with the wind

I know once upon a time I danced and spun and grew
But something stopped all the clocks
And now I don't know what to do

I'm coated in layers of dust and decay
The leaves they rattle by
I'm feeling rather stuck and spent
Perhaps one day I'll move again
On a day that's heaven sent

Until that dawn
My eyes are open
Forced to stay awake
Waiting for the time
When finally this madness I shake.

Oh So Delicate

There's something
So funny to me
That roses are looked at
As weak
Pretentious
Old-fashioned

When they manage to have standards
Where so many of us
Choose to stay silent

Roses are extremely delicate
And die at the signs of disease
But don't we all wish
At the end of the day
We were handled a little bit more carefully?

I Want Everything

How could I not
Long to wash up on foreign shores

How could I not
Want to dance on the top of mountains

How could I not
Wish to kiss every star in the sky

How could I not
Look at the world as our own personal playground

When there are so many colors in the sunsets
And rocks along the shore
Quiet afternoon teas
And gardens dripping with magic

Every book
Every song
Every movie

Taught me there is so much adventure
if you just learn to look.

Stargazer

I'm a pirate ship
Lost at sea
Thoughts of treasure long since faded
Gold coins as worthless as the water around me

The deck is dreadfully empty
Crew long gone
The gun powder all burned down to nothing
Cannonballs now as intimidating as children's toys
Candles melted down to stubs
Darkness washes aboard
Seawater pours from my eyes
I am guided by the stars
To a land I have only dreamed of

I'm a pirate ship
Lost at sea
Siren song pulls at me
There is no sign of shore.
But something in me
Keeps whispering to push on
Navigating
Off nothing than the stars
My tiny signals of hope
Blinking in the sky.

Cliffside

Have you ever stood at the edge of insanity?
Knowing one tiny step and you'll be lost in it
Flying through the air
Pitching forward
To finally meet your destiny

It's always felt inevitable
These feelings too big
My head too small
My heart too bitter

What
Holds me back
From losing it all?

One small little step
Between here
And there

If you've ever stared down the bend
And been breaths from forgetting yourself
You'll understand
The rush
The fear
The pain
That comes with being someone too close to the edge.

Diary of an Almost

There are days I regret not going to school for mortuary science

I feel a deep need to honor the dead
To treat their final moments above ground with tenderness and respect
To brush their hair like their mothers used to
Do their makeup to mimic the glimmer their soul held inside

I want to know they are cared for
That people aren't afraid of them,
That near their last earth-side seconds,
Their hands were held tight, cherished, seen
If only for a moment and by a complete stranger

Their empty shells
These snuffed out candles that held the souls we most adored
Like dwindling smoke
This too will be the last second they're visible

People say they're afraid of Graveyards
But what they mean is they're afraid to one day be buried alone
People say they're afraid of dead bodies
But what they mean is they miss the souls that departed from them so much that to look at what's left behind is worse than seeing nothing and no one at all.

I feel a deep need to honor the dead.

Sugar Pie Honey Bunch

Honeyed words
False hopes

Unhappy cures
Tired tropes

Ghosts of songs linger in the air
Stale sugar still fading from my tongue

Carnival lights blinking
Rides twirling
Kids shouting and shrieking
Signs flashing

To feel sad in a land of technicolor daydreams seems
Just my speed these days
I'm waiting for the top of the Ferris wheel to spin around again.

Starshine

I feel like I've swallowed a Star
Brightness inside me shines out
My heart pumps off pure energy
Starlight beams out of my eyes
My body stretches the cosmos
The inside of me twinkles and glitters
Burning so bright
The thing about stars is
The brighter they burn
The faster they collapse into themselves
I wonder how much time stands between me and complete
devastation

Echoes

At times I worry I'm nothing more than an echo

A figure skater going round and round

A ticking piece of a clock

Maybe I'm just an echo of a girl lived long ago
Simply repeating her movements
Tracing her patterns
Picking up the pain she dropped

A figure skater
Unafraid of ice
Simply trying to get the motions right
Long past the point of stopping

A quiet click clock-ing
Ticking right along
Gear to gear to gear to gear
Hand in hand dragged along through the same old pathways
Following the ruts from feet before mine

I worry I'm nothing but an echo
My thoughts, each one, thought before
My fears imprinted in the framework of me
Never able to say words that haven't already been said

2JUMP

My heartbeat is thrumming in my ears again
Hummingbird fast
Hammering erratically

My thoughts run away with me
My stomach in my toes
Swooping
Soaring
I look out over the ravine
Its river raging
As fast as the pulse in my throat

Each beat brings me one step closer
Each tired moment and pasted smile
I wonder when I will finally jump
And see if I fly like a bird.

Warning Symbols

There is power
In my fluttering skirt hem
And knowledge
Tucked into my curls
There is mystique
Painted onto my lips
The curve of my wrist is a delicacy
And the way I tilt my head a masterclass
My neckline could sink ships
And I control armies
With my gaze
There is danger in being a woman
There is danger to all who meet us.

Radically Alive

I want radical kindness
To love loudly

I used to think my life was for accomplishing goals
To be important
I was living my life off a checklist
Then I got older, and now?

Now I don't care about success
Being famous
Being wealthy
I care about kindness

I want to be warm
Someone who makes you feel
Loved and safe
Seen and valued

I want to relish the mere act of being alive

I want to give love freely and joyously
Because it costs nothing but adds absolutely everything

I no longer care for climbing the ladder
Exhausting myself for work
Measuring myself through productivity
I want to value people more than promotions
I want healthy relationships and communication
All deeply rooted in kindness and care

I want to quietly live a life worth living

Being warm in all senses of the word.

I want radical loving kindness.

Holy Palmers Too

You are holy
Your reserved eyes track me across the room
Your palms face up
Open
Waiting
Guiding me back to you

Eyes glistening
You look at me through stars
The way I've always read about in books but didn't think could be conveyed through glance alone
Now I know holy spaces
I don't dare return to normal ones
I only walk on hallowed grounds.

Heavy

These bones are tired
These are trying times
My eyes have watered
All these flowers and vines

These tears have seeped out of my heart
Landing on the pile

I am fraught.

Nothing Left for You

A cute boy smiled at me in a coffee shop today
and instead of smiling back
I dropped into a bitch face and looked at him sharply,
then turned away.
It was my gut reaction.
It was my instinct.
And I startled myself
because
before I had smiled at every woman,
at every child
that had walked by me in this busy coffee shop I had been loitering
in for half an hour.
I instantly responded with a smile to them,
but to him I shut down.
And then he was gone in an instant,
walking by,
and I tried to catch his eye
too late to smile back
and properly respond,
to apologize with my eyes
and offer back what he so freely gifted me.

I wanted to stop him,
to grab his hand
and explain
that somehow
every smile seems like an invitation to hurt me
and how every man can seem like a weapon walking by
for me to politely move around and not provoke.

I wanted to smile at him and give him a tiny piece of my soul that
wasn't bitter yet,
wasn't jaded by doubt and self-protection.

But he was already out the door.
The moment was over.
And I don't know if I had any smiles to give anyway.

Drunk Girls in A Bathroom

We tuck knives in our lacy socks
And we keep keys between our fingers
Our Mace matches our nail polish
alarms inside our handbags

We are hunted in the streets
We are taught to become trackers
Every man
And every corner
A threat
The edges of my eye
Keeping watch in the night

No one protects women like a woman
I've never held a bond like those with my sisters
Unspoken truths passed between drunk small talk in a bathroom stall
Compliments given out like candy
Hushed warnings passed from lips to ears
There's nothing you'll ever see
Like a woman with her war smile on.

Paths divulged in a wood, right?

There's a moment
Full of stillness
When you feel your heart in your throat
And the air doesn't even dare move
Caught in terror of the crossfire

And you feel yourself at a crossroads
Where only one path leaves with you still on speaking terms
But no matter which you choose
You'll walk hand in hand with devastation on the way

You feel words bubbling up your throat
You know the ice is getting thinner
All you can do now
Is tell the truth
and hope the forest recedes soon
Because the light is dim
The birds are silent
The storm is near

I've read about these
Paths before
But I see no yellow woods
The colors leached away
I can only hope to see you
On the other end
I can only hope you stay.

Don't Wake the Beasts

Sometimes I lay and watch the sun create shadows and whirls on my ceiling
My little patch of grass
In a big big world
And the hours tick on by
There's many a thing I should have done
And instead I do simply nothing at all
Praying and staring at the ceiling
Day in and day out and day in and day out and day in and and and

The world creeps ahead
And I stay the same
The tides ebb and flow
And I stay the same
The moon waxes and wanes
And I stay the same

I know the cracks in the ceiling and the divots in my hips and the way the curtain flutters and the way the light looks soft in the morning and faded at night

I know all this
From my tiny tiny spot
I'm trapped in amber
A fossil that didn't pass
Living dead girl
Breathing already gone girl
Eyes open asleep girl

I am quiet
I don't make a sound
Don't wake the beasts
Who scurry all around

Just watch the ceiling
Dream of the sky
Watch the lights flicker and flicker on by

Witches

I have a secret
Girls are magic

Girls hold the universe in their palms

They say they burned witches at the stake
But what they didn't realize
Was all women hold magic in their cores
Built
Fueled
Boiled
From the inside out

It drenches everything we touch
We weave worlds out of words
Threads pulled tight together
Linking and twisting and bending
To create entire kingdoms
Entire galaxies
Out of nothing more than relationships
Scraps of cloth
And smiles

You can no more burn the magic out of us
Than you can define it.

Chilled to My Bones

Some days I feel like I'm losing my mind
Slipping round the bend
The world lit only by moonlight
Sunshine a distant memory
Warmth gone
Chilled to my bones

I feel like I'll never be happy again
Like I'll forever be in this hazy twilight
Not blessed enough to even see the stars
Those pinpricks of hope
Something I've only read about in storybooks
I'm listing
I'm left
I'm lost

Honey & Moonlight

Maybe I will survive this after all
Maybe there is light beyond this mountain
Maybe
Just maybe
Somehow there is a life waiting for me beyond this valley of night
Perhaps something good

Maybe happiness is still steeped in this water
Maybe somehow, I'm wrong
And it will all be worth it

Maybe
The heaviness of the world
Is not a noose
But perhaps instead
A weighted blanket

Maybe my life
Will be full of honey and moonlight again.

Daylight

Throughout my daily life I realize I love to marvel at things.

I marvel at the beauty of the sky
The kindness of my friends
The complexity of music theory
The astonishing thing melody can be.

I marvel at the ripples on the pond
And the leaves twirling in the air,
The grass poking its head out of the ground.
At the sound the wind makes
How softly the sun kisses my face
As its creeping light filters in through my curtains.

I love the way my shoes sound when I walk
How melodic your laugh sounds against the hardwood floors
The way a book feels in my hand.

I'm constantly astonished and awakened by the things around me.
I love to love.
And I'm terrified that one day, I won't be.

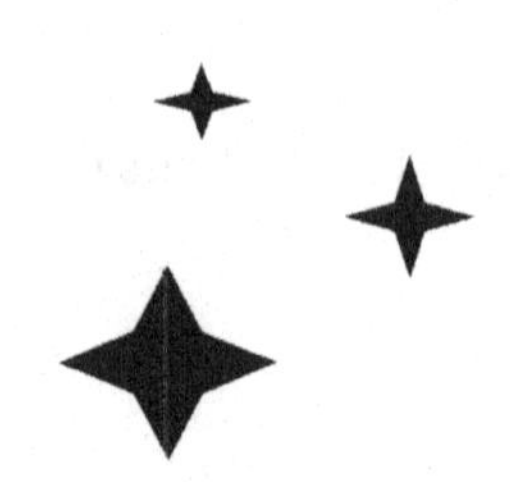

& Then

End Credits

You smell tired
Your eyes are cloudy
Your fingers are splayed
Across the countertop
Where we have shared hours and hours of laughs and tears

The air feels stagnant
Soupy and full of smoke
We both know the credits will roll soon
And this chapter will be over
The only ones to remember us
Will be the stars in the sky
Who saw the moments slip by

You look defeated
I feel detached
The sheen of the day has worn to nubs
I hate goodbyes
My hair has knots
And you smell tired

Our hands brush farewell.

Demanding Little Headstrong Girl

I was born yearning
Screaming full blast
Trying to communicate
My shock and awe
From day one I've blinked into this brightness
Feeling just a little adrift

Smoke & Mirrors

I've never felt an anger
Like I held when I was 15

There's nothing like that stage
Waiting in the wings for your freedom

You hold no autonomy yet
Other than that which you ripped away
Clenched between ice cold shaking hands
Unsure of how you can be so cold
And have such rage
Locked inside your throat

Smoke unfurls
From me
Leaking into everything I say
Black curling rage
Spills out of every orifice

Too much hate to hold
I spend a lot of my time
Screaming at the sky

The birds long know
This is no place for them
There's no silence in these hills
Only ragged offerings
To what seems like a vengeful god

I'm full of acid
Corroded with it
I've forgotten what it's like
To see without the haze of rage
Red tinging the edges of my eyes

Lightning

There was a distinct moment
When I knew I would never love you

Over coffee
In the sunbeam
Your head tilted just so

I wanted it
In that moment
More than anything

To not have this rage
Inside my throat
Curling and choking

But I knew
In that moment
When lightning struck

That I would never forgive and forget
Any more than you
Could apologize

Bonfire Memories

I knew this wouldn't work
When the scent of your skin
Burned in my nose

Acidic
An undercurrent of warning
Like a poisonous plant's bloom

Tempting, a little beautiful
Yet repulsive

I wanted to reach for you
But the warning lingering in the air
Kept my hands tied to my sides
My heart beating
My head swimming
Confused

Everything made sense on paper
Yet
Felt just a bit off
Distorted like a funhouse mirror

My heart flipped on itself
Unsure of want

Part of me wanted to run to you
Part of me wanted to run from you

I guess in the end
With my feet locked to the ground
They made the choice for me.

I couldn't push myself towards you
That leap too great to cross

When the smell of warning lingered
Like a bonfires memory on my skin

Tightropes

When I was a little girl
I used to go out into the road
And tightrope walk
Between the yellow lines

I knew the rule
Was to not cross
The thick painted cautionary yellow
The two lines running side by side
Never touched
Parallel
Severe
And strong

So I knew in the middle
Of those big lines
That neutral space
The
Tiny
Tiny
Strip in the middle was safe

Because you cannot cross the lines
If you were not me
Dancing down the road in the smallest forbidden space
Nestled between lines of traffic

I trusted so completely
So fully
In my safety
In the rule that no one crosses the big yellow lines

It never occurred to me to be scared or worried or alarmed

Whenever a car came I delighted in the rattling my bones made
The wind as it blew back my hair
The air as it whisked up leaves
The thrum in my chest from the metal beast

Passing so close to me
Yet so far away
I never knew I was prey

I had no fear in my small soul
Because to me that space was for dancing
Not cars

I miss that naivety
Where I thought no one could touch me
Because the rules said not to
I miss that optimism
That people would do as they're told
I miss that trust
Where I believed
Nothing could get me

The most natural thing in the world was to walk that tightrope line
down the center of the road

Off

Off on an adventure
I just hadn't found yet
That I knew had already begun

Left Wondering

You speak to me like I'm already gone
Your words already trapped in amber and immortalized before they reach my ears
What about me leads you to think I'm leaving
I wonder
Not realizing I'm in the process
Of being left

Blood Pressure

Those nights where your blood races just under your skin
Your breath catches again and again
Your body on high alert
Waiting
Waiting
Waiting

For what?

Rotting Teeth

Once upon a time I fell in love
Well it only lasted a few seconds
And it wasn't quite love
But it was something close
Something nearby
A neighbor perhaps
A fond likeness
A thrilled affection
A happy concern for
Something along those lines

I fell in like
And when I fell in fondness
For this boy
With deep dark hair
And dark deep eyes
I forgot to look further

It only lasted but a minute
In fact, perhaps just a second
Where I convinced myself
Willed myself
Pushed myself
Wanted myself to be in like
No -- in love
With this boys laugh and crooked smile and haunted eyes

And I tried
And I said it back
I said those words
I whispered I love you too

But before that I tried to give myself an out and I said, "are you sure?"
That simple question ringing in my soul like a phone left off the hook
The term feeling off-kilter bestowed upon my shoulders, I felt the words hit me and shrunk about three inches
The I love you sitting like an itchy sweater, a bit comforting but mostly irritating-
I said "are you sure"
I asked
mostly hoping for reconsideration
And yet he persisted
Yes, he loved me.
He's happier than he's ever been
That's when I notice I feel a tad bit hollow

And I told myself that my racing heart thumping like a bunny with its leg caught in a trap was normal
That it was a common symptom of love
That lovesickness must be described by pounding heart and distrustful eyes

I told myself I was just nervous
Just young
Just silly
Just not appreciative
I told myself I loved this boy like the light from the sun

But then I remembered I much prefer night to day
Much prefer
moon to sun
Much prefer dark to light

I let myself be aware of my distaste for the way he held my hand-
Like it was settling on a pair gloves that happened to be on sale and
not like the gift you've been eyeing all holiday season
Like it was obvious and not a surprise

I let myself remember I wanted more than this
These late-night trysts and kisses that felt misplaced, meant for
someone else
I let myself remember I wanted more than glass half full, or being
thankful for a glass at all- I wanted it fucking overflowing
I wanted a stream,
No, I wanted a river
No, I wanted a waterfall
A rainstorm of love so huge and undeniable that I am swept away
Like Noah on an ark
Completely undeniable
Swept away
Pushing forward to somewhere I've never been before
into uncharted territory

Swept away to a place
Of love and happiness
That didn't feel stolen
Or make me feel like I'm
Lying through my teeth every time I smile
The lies settling between my teeth like sugar and rotting me From
the inside out

I remembered
I remembered
And I realized this was a wrong fit
Like a wrong turn
Down an unfamiliar
Unwelcoming road

I said again "are you sure"
Because I knew
I knew he would reassure me before he opened his lips
And when he did the metallic taste of disappointment
Mistrust
And sadness welled up inside me

I smiled
I bared my rotting teeth
And I let him kiss me
I knew I was leaving
This was a kiss goodbye
I was on my way out the door

I knew
I knew
That I would not stop until I found that waterfall
Until I was swept away in a storm
Until I didn't feel like a settlement
Until I felt like a prize.

Tombstones

I'll haunt the graveyards
I'll weep
I'll wail
I'll haunt these graveyards
I'll leave a trail
These hallowed grounds bring me peace
I've never been scared to rest here
These spirits surround me with love and with care
I am the loudest girl in this land
The trees and the tombstones never share my secrets
Unlike people I've called friend
The dust doesn't linger here
The leaves skitter by quietly
Leaving me to find the peace I've craved since I was a girl

Small

You grabbed my shoulders
And my heart fell

You grabbed my shoulders
And in that moment, I felt small.

I don't usually feel small.
I walk among giants daily.
Sure, their steps might be wider
But I'm steady

In the end, that's what matters.
But when your hands were digging into my skin
I suddenly felt
Very very small

The vulnerabilities I cloak in lipstick and perfume
Instantly apparent under the harsh fluorescent lights

I knew in that moment
You could see the hairline cracks
In my face
The poison at the edges of my heart
The rot in my soul
The hurt in my hands
The ache in my stomach

I knew that my tricks and facade weren't working
Like the lights full blast inside of a theatre
The mystique was gone.

I felt small.
I felt hollow.

And you held my future in your hands so casually.
Maybe you didn't know
My breath was bated

Envelopes Handled with Care

I wish I could fold myself up
Slide into an envelope
And mail myself to you

Shuffling along with other words of love and care and sympathy
I am passed
Hand to hand to hand
Until I end up in your palm

Where I could give myself a shake and unfold
Only to fold you into my arms

Eclipse

I ache with it
This yearning
To see
To do
To be
Everything I dreamed of
To swim amongst the cosmos
And drink the stars
To gorge myself on their light
And finally eclipse the darkness I carry inside me

Stale

The taste of cigarettes
In the back of my throat
The idea as stale as the air between us

Strained and full of smoke
The tension between us broke
As you finally opened your mouth and choked
Out the words that finally ended this ordeal
That never felt quite real
A gauntlet thrown at my feet
Where they laid
Cast off from the palace of your lips
My nerve endings frayed
I took the air in careful sips
As my heart prayed
For this to be a dream

Over the River

Over the river
And through the woods
To grandmothers house we go

When I was a child my grandparents lived next door to us until I was five
Then they moved further away
And to get to their house we had to go the majestic route
Of over the river
Through the woods
To grandmothers house we go

But really
As much as we loved my grandma
We adored my grandpa

We worshipped and lapped at his ankles
Never more than two steps behind
Following him on adventures
Into the forest
Or to check on his chickens

To an animal swap meet, where old men in flannel met up in empty fields and traded animals and stories over burnt cups of coffee wearing their hats depicting which war horrors they bore witness to as young men.

Or maybe just to build something.
We had equal chances going to the library or chasing waterfalls As
we did coming home with a puppy or baby goat
That was a recipe for incandescent chaos as a child.

We never knew exactly where we would end up with Papa, but we
knew we would chew big sticks of pink bubblegum and sing at the
top of our lungs on the van ride there.
Tumbling together in the back seat like puppies
Happy just to be along for the ride.

Acid Rain

Some days the tears are ready to fall at any second for any reason

Pooled behind my lashes

Barely hanging on to decorum

I have this well inside of me
Or maybe it's a geyser

Full of heartbreak and frustration translated into salty tears
Or maybe it's acid rain?

So much a part of me
Yet wrenched away
With the storm

Saltwater

Because my letters to you keep washing up on shore
Ending up miles and miles away from your ears

My words stuck in my throat
Choking in mouthfuls of seawater
Filling my lungs with it
I sink feeling every ounce of oxygen leave my body
My head starts to swim
Here I am suffocating and yet I'm still
Floundering to explain to myself why you are on my mind

I want to forget you
I want these feelings to follow the tide out into the ocean
Drifting by lazily under the summer sun

Instead I drown in my words
I drown in these feelings
Lost among the waves.

Another Sunset

I hope I dream of lovely things
Hugs and kisses, jewel-toned rings
The sun is slipping beneath the fog
Night air creeping ever closer
Sunlight gives me a last kiss goodbye
I feel its lips on the crown of my scalp
The warmth fades so quickly these days

Admit It

It's hard for me
To admit what I want
And I want you
I want you to want me
And I want to want you
And maybe
We can meet in the middle of that want
And stroll hand in hand
To love

Hope for me
was letting myself
Even think of you
And the soft light touching your hair
The way I wanted to

Not the Careful-est of Girls

I am not a graceful girl
I did not grow into a graceful woman
But instead one that crashes into things
Sometimes in a good way sometimes a bad

I was used to hiding
Squishing myself smaller
Wishing
Yearning to be tiny even tinier
To take up less space
Half-moons in my palms from the anxiety of being alive
The grooves deep and sure where my stomach was sick and full of dread

Now I crash into rooms
Bump into chairs and tables
Brush by everyone
Unabashedly here

I consume the space around me
Hungry for it
Taking up as much as possible

Saying yes, I exist
Yes, I'm allowed
Yes, I am here
On full display

I am not a Graceful woman
I am loud
Messy
I have bruises and scars to show it
My body is a map of each gash and each heartbreak
Unashamed and gloriously present.
I no longer exist to be seen
I exist now to see.

Sugar Lies

So, if you jump, I jump
And I jump to conclusions
Together we make
The most uneven pair

Awkward footing
And missed glances
Together yet separate
A glass wall between us
Words of spun sugar in the air

You and I dash just out of reach
Hand grasp and eyes flash
Like I'm at the end of my leash

Angry and stomping and spitting
I twirl I run I leap
From one moment to the next
Leveling entire kingdoms
With my gaze

So you jump and I jump
And we don't say a word
I back up you advance
I leap and you slide
Around and around and around we go
Never too far
But never too close

Toothache

My teeth ache
From holding
These words in
My feet hurt
From sprinting
To meet your ever-mounting expectations

I can feel my pulse thudding in my throat
Heartbeat ratcheting up, up, up

Avoiding your eyes
I lift mine to the heavens
Praying for cloud cover
So I might not be seen so easily.

Say It Again, I Dare You

I've always been someone who wanted "too much"
Expected too much
Felt too much
Loved too much
Hurt too much
Sang too much
Was angry too much

Spent too many days tinged with sadness

Planned too many trips across the world in my head

Was let down by reality

Was told I needed to calm down

Was told I had too high of hopes

Was always overwhelming people

But you know what?
How weak.
That my joy overwhelms you
That my sadness can sink you
That my heart confounds you
That my dreams scare you

No
They are not too much

Because I am captaining and piloting this ship off of the smoke pouring from my ears
Coal can turn to diamonds if you don't get sidetracked by fears

And every time you brush up against me and deem me unworthy, I am reminded to dig my heels in and kick and scream and sing higher and work harder

Because if no one but me can understand the cartography of my heart
Then I must make my own road map
And endure the valleys to get to the mountains
To climb into the sunlight out of the darkness
And paint each cloud in the sky with exact precision
Because I love the way they look
And that will inspire me to keep moving forward
Even when I feel like I'm drowning
In a sea of nerves

But I am sunlight dappled through trees
And raindrops on fall leaves

I am holiday joy and breathless sadness mixed into one
And that's not a bad combination
It's normal to feel both sometimes

I can reflect on my life with love and appreciation like watching a wonderful sunset and still look forward to seeing the stars

Beauty comes in many forms
And I won't allow you to shame me for loving every single one of them

I won't allow myself to be shrunk down to your version of worthy
I won't allow my dreams to be patted on the head and turned away
I will water them
And they will grow
In many directions I didn't know they would
But that's still good

I will not feel out of place because you feel small.

Locket Full of Love

Your face is the kind I would like to keep in a locket around my
throat
Wearing your smile
Close to mine

Maps

Shouldn't I know what we're doing?
Shouldn't I know where this thing is going?
Shouldn't I know when I look in your eyes
What I am thinking
Why is it a surprise

Nothing with us was linear
Every step made me dizzier
Twirling to keep up with your thought process
An exhausted prizefighter stuck still in the ring
Like a breathless ballerina on the tips of her toes

Too bad our dance was never in time
Always out of sync
Like the nauseating calm before a storm we never strike at the same time
Like thunder and lightning
One always chases the other

After all this my emotions are fried
My head is spinning
My lungs are heaving
At first, it's exciting
Never knowing what's going on
But after a while I just keep dreaming of leaving.

Ghost Summer

One day
I want
To grow up
And have a
castle made of thunderstorms
and lightning by the seaside
Some days I think
That I
Am more ghost
Than girl
and more blood
Than guts
And more dreams
Than grit

Poison on Your Lips

I used to hold too much anger
The poison inside me couldn't be contained
I spent years rotting from the inside out
Until I dove deep and dug out the decayed pieces of my soul

I spent years rebuilding
This body I call a home

Spent so many years
Sucking venom from these veins

That I was terrified at the very idea of ever allowing myself to be mad again

A raised voice
A slammed door
A jostled table
Left me skittering
Skin jumping
Muscles clenched
Frozen

I spent so long erasing the impulse to set fire to the room around me
That eventually I had no spark

I forgot how to use my anger at all

Instead I shoved it into a dusty box under the stairs
Adamant to never use it again
Afraid of what bridges I would burn
Afraid of what venom would slip beneath my teeth
What glass would crack underneath my hand

But slowly
So slowly
Imperceptible nearly
I remembered that a little fire is necessary to keep you warm
And my anger too has its place

It's a hard battle
Allowing it to join my table
Without burning my home to the ground

Trusting myself
A hard-fought battle
When I know in the past
I would drink poison
Just to spite your words of warning

Day by day
I play
A game against myself

Some days my voice gets too loud again
And that same old fear darkens my door
But some days my point is made,
My boundaries are set
And I haven't destroyed anything or anyone in the process.
It's a little easier
Every time I try

My hands itch toward the dagger in my back
But I don’t use it
Not anymore.

Nighttime Prayers

Now I lay me down to sleep
I pray the lord my soul to keep
If I should die before I wake
I pray the lord my soul to take
But if I wake
The lord I beg
Help keep me sane
in my dear little head

Deals with the Devil

When you kiss me
Do you know you're sipping poison?
A deal with the devil
A trade you weren't even sure about making
There is witchcraft in my lips.

Kaleidoscope Girl

Sometimes I think I'm a kaleidoscope
Everyone who views me
Sees me a bit different
Than I was the moment just before

I'm constantly shifting
Changing
Evolving
Scattering
Pushing
Shoving
Collapsing into myself
Only to be made anew
Again and again and again

Mad tea cups
Spinning, spinning, spinning
Changing by the second
Into someone new
Based on your perception

I am made of
What I am made of
Yet to you
I'm tilted
Slanted
Curved

Just a bit
Crooked

Quiet Truths

That moment when you're 15 in a CVS and see all the models on the front of magazines and no one looks like you

That sinking of your stomach when you're staring at yourself in clothes that don't fit in a dressing room mirror

The numbness that comes from feeling like you'll never be anyone's first choice

The quiet flatness you feel standing in the bar nursing a drink while people flirt with your friends and you stand there glanced over before it even began

There is disillusionment in being a woman

Some days my skin feels stretched too tight over my bones
My hair is flat, and my skin is dry
But that doesn't mean I'm not beautiful.

Grocery Store Eggs

Over the many seasons of my life
People have told me
I'm too sensitive
That things said are taken too personally
That I should
Grow a backbone
Get some humor
Grow up
Learn to take it
That I'm a wimp
I'm a baby
I can't take a joke

That I'm sensitive.

So, what if I am?
So what if I require a gentler hand?
So what if I am like the eggs you gather at the grocery store-
checked before you pick me up,
carried delicately,
checked again that I have no cracks
before you take me home to rest.

Maybe others can be jostled and nudged and manhandled

Maybe I can't
And so what?

Is that the worst thing to ever happen to humanity?
That my heart requires an extra moment or two of thought before action?
That you consider the way you slant your words to me?

So what if I do?
So what if I am?
Sensitive is not a bad thing
Unless you make it one

Windy Day

I pray and pray and pray.
Tears mixing with the prayers on my lips.
I wonder if anyone hears my whispers
Or if they are simply carried off by the wind
Like a seed looking for somewhere to grow.

Lack of Humor

And you reached for just
A little too much
And you pushed
Just a little too far

And the city lights flashed around us
Romantic moments going sour
Freeze framed
Like a lightning flash
Like the death of a flower

I thought
Oh, I thought
Foolishly so

And then I just knew I had to go
Slow slow slow my heart kicked
And my smile just a little bit
Slipped

Jumbled and jangled
My nerves cracked
This moment so mangled
I could have just laughed

At the irony
At the lack of humor here

Bottles From the Sea

Sometimes talking to you
Feels like putting a message in a bottle
And throwing it out to sea

Sometimes the waves sweep it away
My words never reaching your ears
Words dying on lips
Words made out of my tears

Glass bottles bobbing and weaving
Tossed in and out of waves

Once in a while one washes up
On the tiny island you put yourself on
So far away too far to touch
Just close enough to see

You feel miles and miles from here
My heart beating in time with the waves
I'm watching the sun fall and the moon rise
And I'm thinking of the darkness in your eyes

I wonder what you would say
If you would respond at all

More often than not my glass bottles return to me
Empty
Empty
Empty

Empty Hands

And you chose her.

You looked me dead in the eye
Smiled
And picked up her hand

You saw me reaching
You took one step forward
And you pushed past me

I didn't get it at first
Our eyes locked
You smiled just for me

And you chose her.
You chose her.
And I felt it slam through my chest.

I fell for you
One cold fall day
Underneath the oak trees

We sat covered in leaves
And our voices rose and fell and twirled around our heads
And we smiled and laughed

And you chose her.
It's your right
I want you to be happy
But I thought
You were reaching for me
That your smile was our secret
That our laughs
Were building us a path
To walk down
together
Paved with inside jokes and nights spent
Under the stars

Silly me to think your words
Strung together so elegantly
Like pearls on a golden string
Were only for me

I should have known you were
Testing your script
Your hair a little over your eyes
You smile just a bit crooked
Our jokes always felt like a disguise

You looked me dead in the eye
Smiled
And picked up her hand.

Heavy Hymnals

These hymns feel heavy on my
Lips
A flower of resentment
Blooms inside my throat
Every time I'm told
My clothes are responsible
for someone else's sinful thoughts

Spiderwebs

I see you covering me in spiderwebs
Spinning lies between your teeth
Weaving them with your fingers
Layering the gossamer thin strips over me
Again
Again
Again

Until you can't quite see me underneath
Until
I'm nothing more than your idea of me

Soda

This yearning, this want in my stomach and clammy clutch at my chest
Isn't wholly unwelcome

And that
Is the most alarming part of all

I crave partnership lately
A love to grow
Someone to shower my affections and thoughts on
Someone to hold my hand and grab my purse and read the directions and grab a soda for

I used to be a one woman show
A solo act
But my jokes with you land smoother and our banter wins awards
Maybe the fact you're still here
Says more than you do.

Spit

I'm pulp
Mush
Decimated
By the time you get done
Chewing me up just to spit me out

SEARCHLIGHT

I'm constantly snatching beautiful moments from thin air
Bringing them close
and breathing them in

I'm a source of life
I hold it in me
I hold it to me

These moments spinning like thread out from my fingertips

I gather gather gather them against my chest
Nursing each one
Heaving and clutching
Eyes furiously searching for the next
Scared to lose a single one.

What's My Cue Again?

The first time I ever kissed a boy I was five years old
I kissed Daniel at daycare, up in the wooden play set.
I was not hesitant, or afraid like he was, and I simply leaned in,
fearlessly connected our lips and pulled back, unsure why this
simple act was a way of conveying love.

Everything I did as a child conveyed love.
This act seemed the least of it at the time.

Now crossing those boundaries as an adult seems ever intimidating
and vast.
More than a simple invasion of personal space.

I kissed him and then went to snack time, the imprint of the
moment barely sticking with me as important.
It seemed so effortless to express and connect.
Simple.

My next kiss wasn't for many years, I layered and cloaked myself in
untouchability.

When I was a child I expressed and emoted and screamed my
feelings all at once and all the time.

Sometimes I still feel that way now.
Like I'm endlessly shouting cues to the universe.

Weak Coffee

I said I was fine
But I still think about you

I broke up with you
But I had to sell my car to forget what you sitting next to me looked like
To forget you reaching for me pulling me tight across those seats at every red light
Holding my hand
Opening my door
I had to sell the memories right out from under me

Because no longer could I see
The road ahead of me
No, I was staring straight ahead but still it was the memories behind me that crowded in
I wanted to forget you
But those happy flashes of your hand reaching for mine
And your eyes dancing in the light from the streetlamps
Those I want to keep

But to keep some is to keep it all
And besides shouldn't I want to remember my first fall
After all I leapt head over heels at first
Tumbled over myself to get to you
Threw pride out the window
Pushed ego to the side
Was honest and not careful

God, how I cried
When you left and my fingertips just brushed air
But even when you were there you weren't there

Hugging you was like hugging a ghost
And what I think hurt the most
Was in the end I didn't actually love you
I wanted to
But you were like weak coffee
I couldn't make myself choose you a second time
I wanted to love you
Those bitter words crept past my lips only once
But I could feel the lie crawling on my skin
Burning the back of my throat
Twisting in my stomach

In the end I didn't love you
But god I wanted to.

The End

I have read countless acknowledgement pages in books over the years while I stuffed my head full of fairy tales and love stories, but never did I think I would get to write my own.

This book goes out to everyone I have ever gotten to love, thank you for teaching me what that word means. Whether we walked together for a season or a lifetime you are imprinted on my heart.

To my sweet family and friends for encouraging me that people would somehow care enough to read my thoughts. And thank you to the people who said, "oh, finally!" when I tentatively brought up writing a book.

A special thank you to Rachel Carpenter for being the best editor and sounding board who also happens to have the cutest kittens in all the lands.

To Matthew Z. Gillin for the best notes, drawings, and memes a girl could ever need. Thank you for bringing my cover to life. When I handed you several random pieces and ideas you nodded and did exactly what I dreamed of, because you are magic. Thanks for always understanding me even though 90% of what I say makes no sense. Tall Terror, you truly bring so much light to my life and you're forever loved and appreciated.

Emily Kaye and Megan Aleece thank you for being the sweetest souls to bounce poems off of.

Lizzy Anderson, my forever Teen Queen. Love you always, for all of it.

Jordan Parker Holmes for being my editing buddy. Thanks for laughing at my jokes and singing Hannah Montana with me.

My Mom, Papa, and Grandma for encouraging me to write and sing before I even knew how. Thanks for letting my spirit scream.

None of this writing would live up to my gorgeous cover without these people.

If you read all of this, I hope you find all the magic you're searching for. I hope you never have to stifle yourself and can create your own Crescendo of Chaos, whatever that term means for you, never scared to make a joyful noise.

VICTORIA LAUREN was raised on a steady diet of fairy tales and love songs. She studied opera performance as a dramatic coloratura soprano and cites music as her first love, books as her lifelong affair. She loves travel, collects kitschy antiques, and lives in the Midwest with her three-legged puppy named Valentine.

Crescendo of Chaos is her debut novel.

Made in the USA
Coppell, TX
17 March 2021

51884121R00090